The Cute, the F̶ & the Weird

Journal of Cats

pt 1

This journal belongs to:

_____

Me-ow?

The Cute, the Funny, and the Weird Journal of Cats, pt 1

Created by Katja Vartiainen
2021
ISBN: 9798536724149

https://linktr.ee/katjavartiainen

font: Averia Serif Libre by Dan Sayers (i@iotic.com)

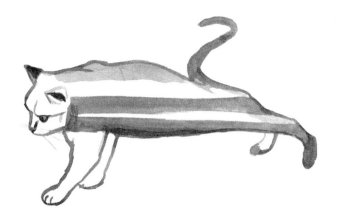

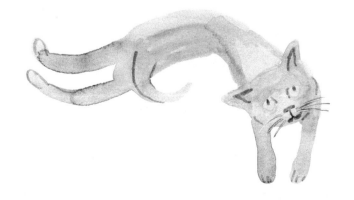

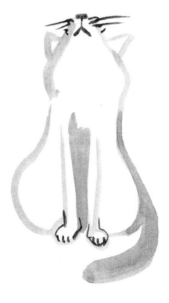

Printed in Great Britain
by Amazon

71475792R00072